DUET DISCOVE

12 Lower Intermediate Pieces for 1 Piano

T0055814

Compiled and Edited by Bradley Beckman and Carolyn True

ISBN 978-1-4803-4541-6

HAL•LEONARD®
CORPORATION
7777 W. BLUEMOUND RD. P.O. BOX 13819 MILWAUKEE, WI 53213

In Australia Contact:
Hal Leonard Australia Pty. Ltd.
4 Lentara Court
Cheltenham, Victoria, 3192 Australia
Email: ausadmin@halleonard.com.au

Contents
in progressive order of difficulty

Duet Discoveries

General Comments

With compositions spanning from the late Baroque through the early 20th century, this eclectic set includes perennial favorites and works by lesser-known composers. *Duet Discoveries* will serve as a guide for students on their ensemble journey. As students advance through the twelve graded pieces in this volume, they will explore a variety of ensemble techniques. The pieces are sequenced taking into account both musical and technical challenges.

Pedaling

When pedaling piano music, several issues need to be addressed including (but certainly not limited to): the character of the piece, the color of the desired sound, the dryness or wetness of the sound, the carry-over of harmonies and/or melodic notes, and the function of rests, fermatas, and other durational indications. While much too often, pianists simply "put down the right foot" and take it off when the moment strikes them, one needs to be conscious of the variety of sounds possible by carefully chosen pedaling. The issue of pedaling is even trickier when dealing with piano duets. One has to take into consideration all of the previously mentioned issues, and add to them, issues of two independent pianists with the capability of playing twice as many notes and voices. Who should pedal, the secondo or primo player? Some believe that the secondo player must always pedal, since they generally are playing the harmonic underpinning. Others believe that the primo should pedal since their part more often requires sustained, singing qualities. We the editors tend to make the decision based on the needs of the piece, alternating as the needs demand—sometimes secondo player pedals, sometimes primo. One simply must explore all options including shifting within a single piece. All of the pedal suggestions are editorial.

Fingering

Fingering is as individual as hands are different. When choosing fingerings, one needs to address the desires of the composer (length and dynamic of note patterns, articulation, other expressive elements), phrasing, geography of the keyboard, and natural and efficient physical motions produced by understanding the parameters of the individual hand: length of fingers, breadth of expanse, girth of the fingers and the palm. There are traditional fingerings that serve most hands and many others that serve one hand extraordinarily well while failing another's hand miserably. In piano duet music there is an additional issue: how close are the left hand of the primo and the right hand of the secondo part and what fingerings can give both players space? Sometimes it is helpful to raise or lower the wrist to avoid hands colliding. All of the fingerings for this edition are editorial suggestions. As with pedaling, pianists must spend time exploring fingering options and coming to a conscious decision for each passage. In this way, the musical goals will always be first and foremost.

Metronome Indications

Out of the twelve pieces in this volume, only Ravel specified a metronome indication. Partners are helped by metronome indications, giving each player a guiding tempo for efficient pre-rehearsal practice. We have attached suggested metronome markings for each duet.

Descriptive Tempo Indications

A musical performance communicates through sound, so next to each speed-based tempo indication, we have added a descriptive tempo indication.

Piano Duet Issues

We use several specific terms when referring to partner play. Four are defined here.

1. Balance and Voice Prioritization: In this volume, balance refers to the relationship between the hands in solo piano playing and between composite secondo and primo parts in duet playing. Voice Prioritization refers to dividing the entirety into the number of independent voices, regardless of hand or part, and ranking them from one (the most prominent) to xxx (the least prominent of the voices present). For example, with four voices, 1 would be the most prominent; 2, the second most prominent; 3, the third most prominent; and 4, the least prominent.

2. Passing Off: Just as in a relay race, duet partners often "pass off" melodic or rhythmic material seamlessly between the two parts.

3. Positioning: Many times players must adapt their wrist height and/or fingering to allow two players to share one keyboard.

4. Average Dynamic: If both parts are marked with the exact same dynamic, it is necessary to consider that the "average dynamic" and prioritize the voices to achieve that atmosphere.

Composer Biographies

Johann Anton André (1775–1842), German composer, music editor, publisher. Due to the scholarly work and the purchase of Mozart's musical papers, André has been dubbed "the father of Mozart research." André's work formed the basis of the Köchel catalog. His family's publishing firm, Musikhaus Andre Musikverlag Johann Andre, is still active.

Anton Bruckner (1824–1896), Austrian composer, organist, pedagogue. Bruckner is known primarily as a composer of symphonic and sacred choral works. Additionally, he was recognized for his improvisatory prowess at the organ.

Leopold Godowsky (1870–1938), Polish-born American composer, pianist. Due to his rotund appearance, and his tireless mentoring of generations of pianists, critic James Huneker called him both "the Buddha of the piano" and "the pianist's pianist." Of the composers in this collection, he is the most prolific composer of piano works.

Maurice Ravel (1875–1937), French composer, pianist. One of history's most colorful orchestrators, Ravel infuses classical forms with a refined forward-looking musical language.

Leander Schlegel (1844–1913), Dutch pianist, composer. Although a Netherland native, Schlegel had one musical foot planted in his homeland and the other in Germany. He was greatly influenced by Schumann, Brahms, and Kirchner and founded the Haarlem Wagner Society.

Hannah Smith (1849–1939), American composer, writer, pedagogue. Smith's instructional book *Progressive Exercises in Sight Reading for the Piano* continues to be an invaluable resource for piano teachers. In addition to her teaching pieces, she wrote two books about music, *Founders of Music* and *Music: How It Came to Be What It Is.*

Fritz Spindler (1817–1905), German composer, pedagogue. Composing many of his over 300 compositions for piano students, Spindler also wrote challenging pieces for chamber ensembles and orchestra. He originally studied theology but quickly shifted his focus to music and teaching.

Robert Volkmann (1815–1883), German composer, voice and piano teacher. Although born in Dresden, Volkmann spent most of his life in Budapest. On a trip to Vienna, he became friends with Brahms. In 1875 Volkmann received a teaching appointment to the National Hungarian Royal Academy of Music where he taught alongside Franz Liszt.

Performance and Practice Notes

Cradle Song from *Miniatures*
Leopold Godowsky

1. In this collection we chose fingerings that are both comfortable and serve the musical sound produced. Godowsky originally wrote his "Cradle Song" with the primo part edited for a C Major Five–Finger position, however, we have made some fingering changes for specific sound qualities. For example, in the primo part the two-note slurs in mm. 17–19 are easily played using 3-2 in the right hand and 1-3 in the left hand.

2. At the beginning of "Cradle Song" there are four voices: the primo melody and three accompanimental voices. Pay close attention to the balance between the hands and the two parts.

3. In mm. 16–20, there is an inexact canon and a supporting melody. Prioritize the three melodic lines higher than the secondo part bass voices.

Little Piece No. 1 from *Three Little Pieces*
Anton Bruckner

1. It may seem counterintuitive to mark repeated notes legato. One can get fussy with fingering choices (changing a finger per note), but regardless of fingering, the most important issue is the length of the quarter note.

2. Carefully prioritize all four voices in this "Little Piece." There are many options, so experiment to find the quality of sound to clearly communicate the musical texture.

3. Notice the phrase endings in mm. 8, 16, and 24 are quarter notes followed by two beats of silence. Release the quarter notes gently but in time, and listen to the two beats of silence.

Ariette from *Miniatures*
Leopold Godowsky

1. Godowsky marked half-note pedals throughout this piece; however, with a legato touch the voices will be both beautifully sung and clear.

2. Experiment with different voice prioritizations on the repeats.

3. Godowsky marks accents in the primo melody (mm. 10, 11, 13, and 15). Be careful to add the stresses yet retain the lyrical character of the "Ariette."

Cradle Song from *Four Little Hands*, Op. 20, No. 1
Hannah Smith

1. Gently move the eighth notes of the secondo part forward in a flowing, unhurried manner.
2. The primo part is deceptive. Smith sets each hand in a major five-finger pattern, but quickly expands beyond that. The editorial fingerings will facilitate ease of position changes.
3. Balance the melodic primo part with the accompanimental secondo part.

Little Lullaby from *The Children's Colorful World*, Op. 27, No. 1
Leander Schlegel

1. In 2/4 meter, feel one main pulse per measure. In "Little Lullaby" this will keep the music swaying.
2. In the primo part, mm. 22 and 24, the two hands rhythmically overlap. Experiment with releasing the quarter note as late as possible to retain the character and place within the dynamic swell (m. 22) and decay (m. 24).

ABC from *The Morning*, Op. 39, No. 2
Robert Volkmann

1. Play the eighth notes in a light and bouncy manner to contrast with the more deliberate quarter notes.
2. Enjoy the musical joke in mm. 11–13 by gradually slowing down to the fermata and playing immediately in tempo where marked.
3. Notice that in the primo part (mm. 7 and 9, beat 3) there is a shared F with a melodic purpose (right hand) and a harmonic purpose (left hand). How do you communicate both aspects of the F?
4. Bounce for graceful repetitions (eighth notes in m. 2) in contrast with a staccato touch (mm. 15–17).

Pavane of the Sleeping Beauty in the Forest from *Mother Goose*
Maurice Ravel

1. In this piece, every four measures is a macro phrase. The micro phrases are delineated by articulation marks, just as punctuation helps clarify ideas within a sentence.
2. Some fancy footwork may alleviate pedaling issues. Clearly, the secondo player should pedal the first four measures; however, the *portato* notes in the primo part will be easier to control if the primo player is pedaling. Experiment with the secondo player pedaling mm. 1–4 and mm. 9–12 and the primo player pedaling from mm. 5–8 and mm. 13–the end. Explore variations in depth and length of pedals for each part.
3. The secondo player may want to add *una corda* mm. 17–20 for a different color.

Piano Duet from *Twelve Progressive Pieces*, **Op. 44, No. 7**
Anton André

1. Avoid tangled fingers and hands in m. 15 by carefully positioning the wrists (secondo, r.h. above; primo, l.h. below) and playing all sixteenths with economy of motion.

2. Clarify both the micro and the macro phrases with accurate articulation and the shaping of the long lines.

3. When setting the tempo, remember to use both tempo words as aids: *Andante* (in particular helpful for the sixteenth notes) and *moderato* (thinking one main pulse per measure).

Immortelle in G Major from *Immortellen*, **Op. 90, No. 2**
Fritz Spindler

1. We suggest a shallow pedal to enrich the sound yet avoid blurriness. Listen to how the depth of the pedal changes the sound.

2. To create the same sound on different pianos the actual depth may change. Remember the piano teacher's adage, "Pedal with your ears, not your feet."

3. Clarify both the micro and macro phrases.

Little Piece No. 2 from *Three Little Pieces*
Anton Bruckner

1. Maintain the bouncy quality of the repeated notes by using a light touch.

2. Both the balance between parts and the prioritization of the voices change within "Little Piece No. 2." Where and how?

3. In order to comfortably play a third apart in m. 9 (secondo, r.h. and primo, l.h.), adjust the position of the wrists.

On the Rocking Horse from *The Children's Colorful World*, **Op. 27, No. 3**
Leander Schlegel

1. To avoid a monotonous sound on the repeated notes, alternate fingers for a change of color.

2. Pass off the sixteenth notes between the secondo and primo parts (mm. 9–12) while retaining the primo melody's prominence.

3. Schlegel's programmatic description "the horse falls down" indicates both a volume and a tempo adjustment at the end.

Little Piece No. 3 from *Three Little Pieces*
Anton Bruckner

1. For the first time in this collection, page turning is an issue. If the secondo player's two parts are redistributed as bracketed in the score and played with the left hand, the right hand will be free to turn the page.

2. A musical breath is an unmeasured amount of time as compared with the rhythmic value of a rest. Natural breathing is best served at the end of the mm. 12 and 18.

3. There is an extremely long phrase in "Little Piece No. 3" (mm. 23–30). Sometimes, as in this phrase, the peak is not the highest pitch. Where is the peak of this phrase?

4. There are overlaps in mm. 33 and 49 that are aided this time by the positioning of specific fingers. The primo has a repeated 2-5 fingering. Adjust the height of the 5 to move out of the secondo player's way.

Cradle Song
from *Miniatures*

Leopold Godowsky
(1870–1938)

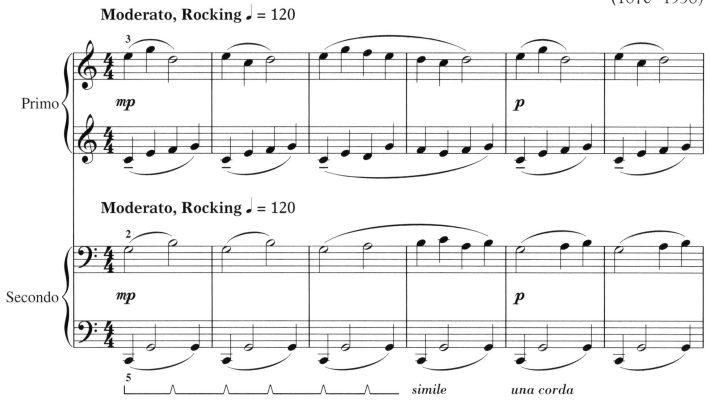

tre corde

una corda

*Voice canon entrance
**Voice in relation to canon in primo

Little Piece No. 1

from *Three Little Pieces*

Anton Bruckner
(1824–1896)

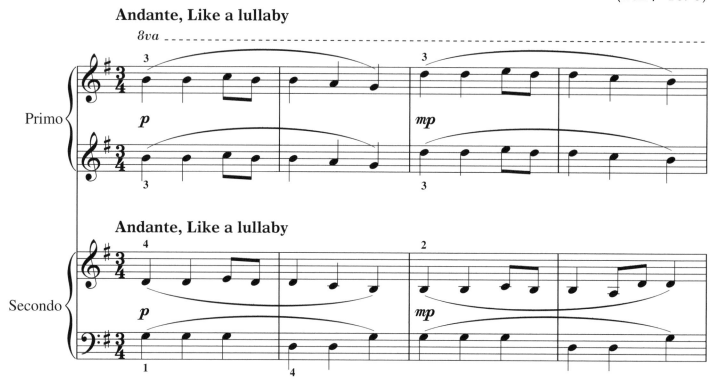

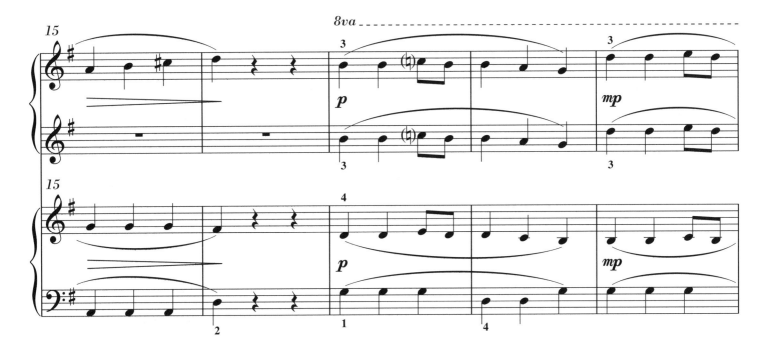

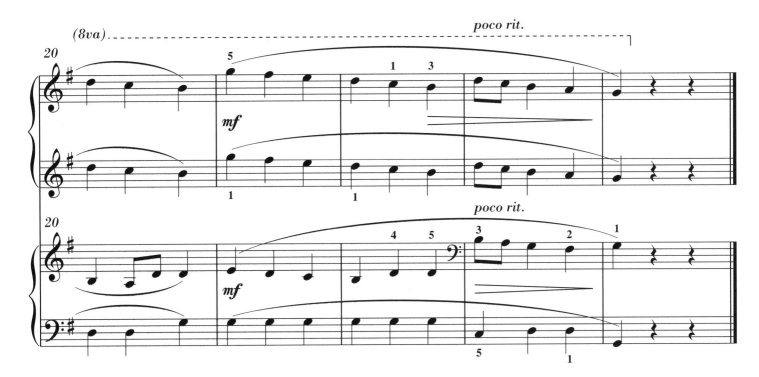

Ariette

from *Miniatures*

Leopold Godowsky
(1870–1938)

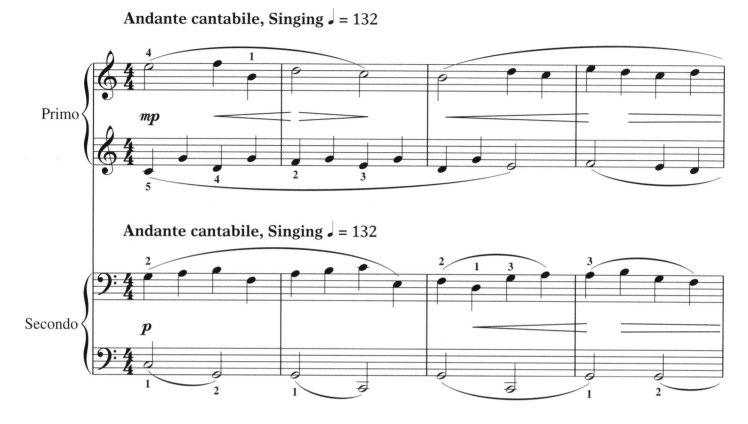

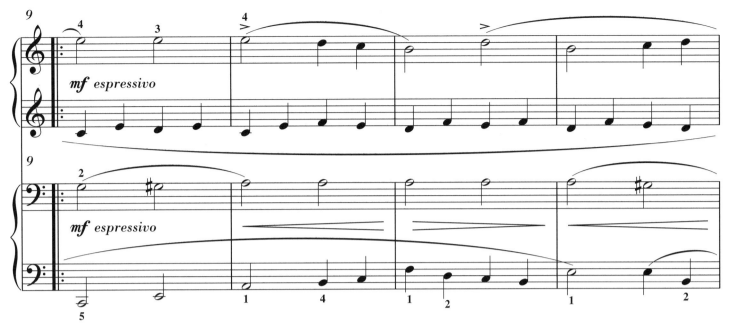

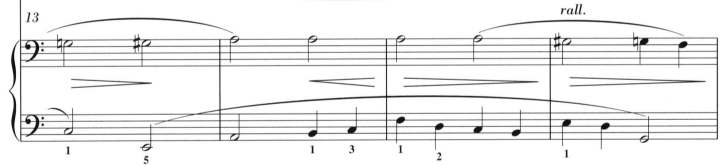

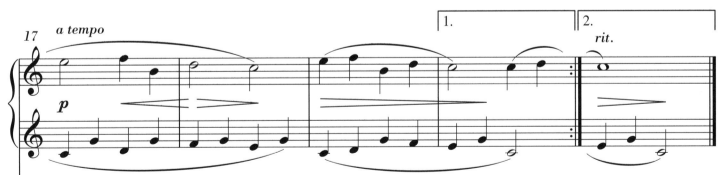

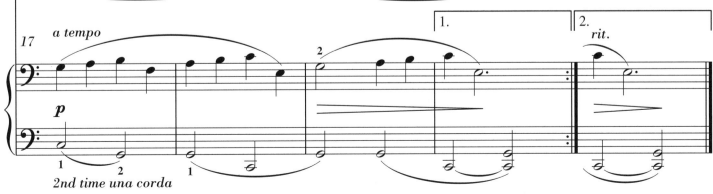

Cradle Song
from *Four Little Hands*, Op. 20, No. 1

Hannah Smith
(1849–1939)

Little Lullaby

from *The Children's Colorful World*, Op. 27, No. 1

Leander Schlegel
(1844–1913)

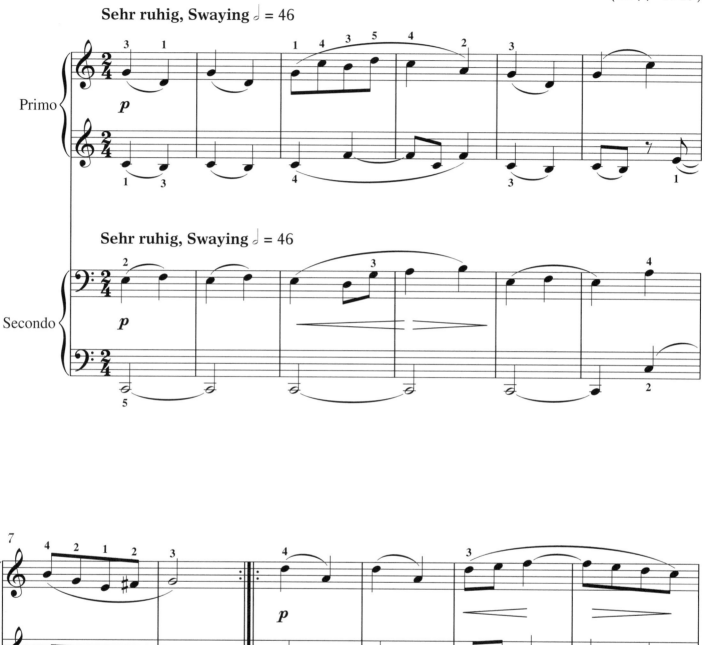

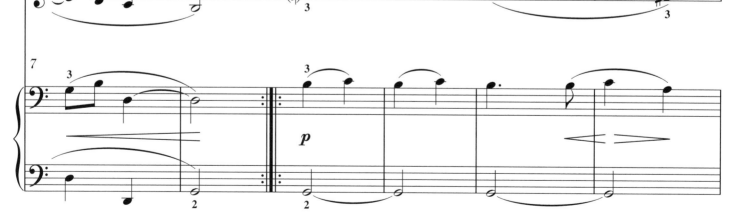

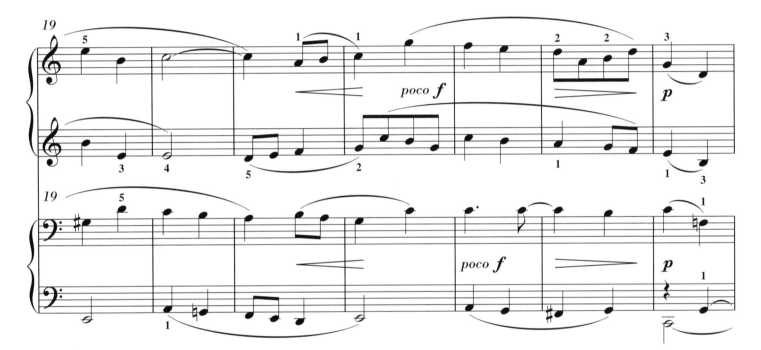

A B C

from *The Morning*, Op. 39, No. 2

Robert Volkmann
(1815–1883)

Pavane of the Sleeping Beauty in the Forest

from *Mother Goose*

Maurice Ravel
(1875–1937)

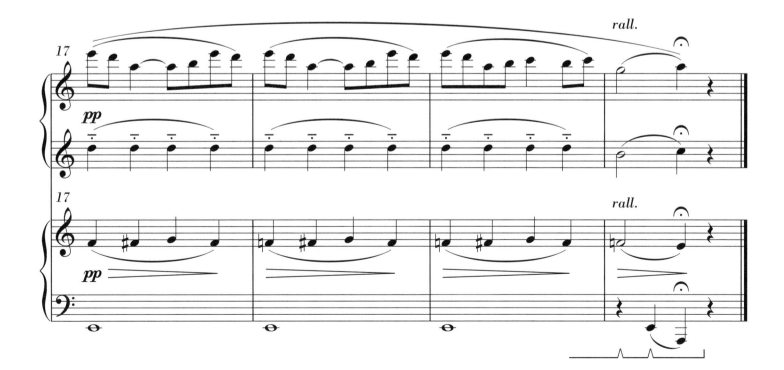

Piano Duet

from *Twelve Progressive Pieces*, Op. 44 No. 7

Anton André
(1775–1842)

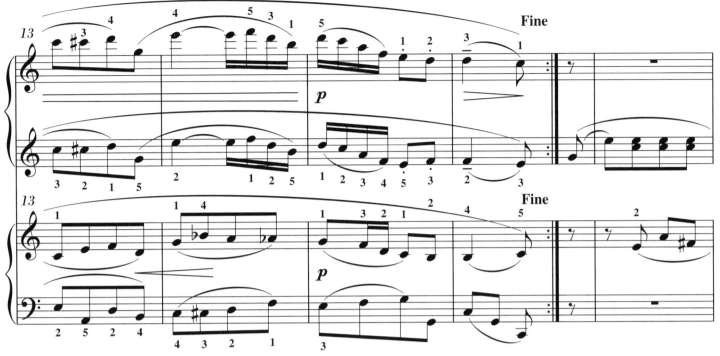

Fine

D.C. al Fine

Immortelle in G Major

from *Immortellen*, Op. 90, No. 2

Fritz Spindler
(1817–1905)

Little Piece No. 2

from *Three Little Pieces*

Anton Bruckner
(1824–1896)

On the Rocking Horse

from *The Children's Colorful World*, Op. 27, No. 3

Leander Schlegel
(1844–1913)

the horse falls down…

the horse falls down…

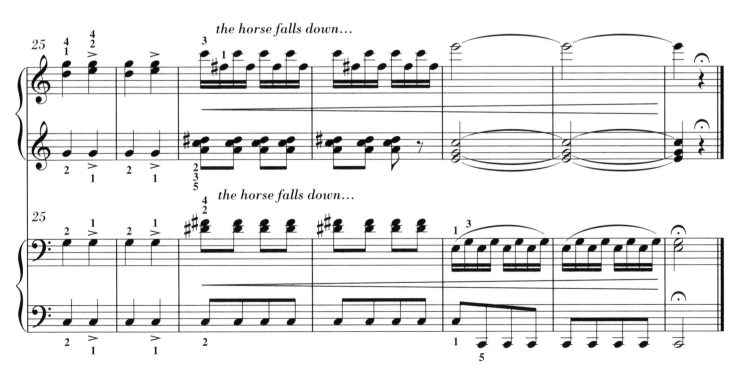

Little Piece No. 3

from *Three Little Pieces*

Anton Bruckner
(1824–1896)

(2nd time RH turn page)

About the Compilers/Editors

The **Beckman/True Duo** has been performing together since 2000 in national and international venues. Presenting both standard and contemporary works from 1900 to present day, their programs include music for duo pianos and piano duet. Their first Duo Piano CD *Bradley Beckman & Carolyn True 2* contains the works of Barber, Bernstein, and Piazzolla. Committed teachers, Beckman and True's collaboration has extended into workshops for experienced teachers and young musicians.

Bradley Beckman is originally from Harvard, Illinois, and received his bachelor of music degree from Illinois Wesleyan University in 1986. While at IWU Dr. Beckman studied with Lawrence Campbell received numerous competitive scholarships, was an Honors Recitalist, and was selected for Pi Kappa Lambda membership. Continued study with Joseph Banowetz brought Dr. Beckman to the University of North Texas in 1986 where he earned both a master of music degree and a doctor of music degree in Piano. While at UNT Dr. Beckman held a competitive Teaching Fellowship in Piano and received the Mary M. Morgan Dissertation Award for Excellence in Music Performance for his work on Ronald Stevenson's *Passacaglia on DSCH*. Dr. Beckman is currently Principal Lecturer in Piano and Group Piano Coordinator at the University of North Texas. He teaches Piano Pedagogy, Keyboard Skills classes, and is faculty advisor for the UNT/TMTA Collegiate Student Chapter. Dr. Beckman has performed throughout the Midwest, is a frequent adjudicator, and has contributed to *Keyboard Companion Magazine* regarding the teaching of adult students. He has been active in Music Teachers National Association and Texas Music Teachers Association as Presenter, Performance Contest Coordinator, Elected Director, and past President of the Plano Music Teachers Association. TMTA chose Dr. Beckman as their Collegiate Teacher of the Year in 2010. Dr. Beckman has performed at the State Department in Washington, D.C., as part of the State of the Arts concert series where his playing was described as "sensitive, well constructed and erupting in a flood of emotions..." (*State Magazine*, Washington, D.C.). He also performs regularly with two-piano partner, Dr. Carolyn True of Trinity University. In 2011 they released their first CD together entitled *Bradley Beckman & Carolyn True* 2. Dr. Beckman is a member of the College Music Society, European Piano Teachers Association, and the American Liszt Society.

Hailed as "an artist with commanding technique, always at the service of the music and capable of taming any tigers the composer has unleashed" (*San Antonio Express-News*), **Carolyn True** is a pianist equally at home on the concert stage and in the teaching studio. A member of the music faculty of Trinity University, True teaches individual lessons, accompanying, piano ensemble, piano literature, piano pedagogy, and other related courses. A compassionate and challenging professor, True is carrying on the family tradition. In 2000, True was recognized as the Texas Music Teachers Association's Collegiate Teacher of the Year and in 2010 was awarded the highest honor to a faculty member at Trinity University, the Dr. and Mrs. Z.T. Scott Faculty Fellowship award. Dr. True holds the prestigious Performer's Certificate and a D.M.A. degree from the Eastman School of Music, an M.M. from the University of Maryland-College Park, and the B.M. from the University of Central Missouri. She was a prize-winner in national and international competitions. She was also the recipient of a Rotary Foundation Scholarship for study at the Conservatoire National de la Musique in Lyon, France. Her CD, *Carolyn True 1*, features works of Ligeti, Bach/Brahms, Beethoven, and Bennett. She has edited two volumes of intermediate piano works by Starer (*Sketches in Color*) and Milhaud (*A Child's Loves*). In addition to her solo and duo work, she is a core member of the award-winning SOLI Chamber Ensemble, the resident chamber ensemble of Trinity University. In 2013 their mission to promote contemporary music to audiences of all ages resulted in the ASCAP/CMA Award for Adventurous programming.